The Importance of Being Ernest
a collection of essays & poetry, 1997 – 2001

&

by Ernest Cline

Write Bloody Publishing
America's Independent Press

Austin, TX

WRITEBLOODY.COM

Cline, Ernest.
1ˢᵗ edition.
ISBN: 978-1938912-30-6

Interior Layout by Lea C. Deschenes
Cover Illustration and Design by Gary Musgrave
Author Photo by Dan Winters
Interior Illustrations by Len Peralta, www.lenperalta.com
Proofread by Helen Novielli
Edited by Derrick Brown and Cristin O'Keefe Aptowicz
Type set in Bergamo from www.theleagueofmoveabletype.com

Printed in Tennessee, USA

Write Bloody Publishing
Austin, TX
Support Independent Presses
writebloody.com

To contact the author, send an email to ernie@ernestcline.com

MADE IN THE USA

THE IMPORTANCE OF BEING ERNEST

THE IMPORTANCE OF BEING ERNEST

INTRODUCTION

I started writing and performing poetry in the mid-90s when I moved to Austin, Texas. I had already tried my hand at both stand-up and improv comedy when I lived in Ohio, but drunk Midwestern comedy club patrons proved not to be the ideal audience for my geeky sense of humor.

Poetry slams – and especially the Austin Poetry Slam – turned out to be a far better fit. Every week I would show up at the late, great Electric Lounge to recite my nerdy three-minute monologues about working a tech support job or loving to play old Atari games. Five randomly selected judges in the audience would rate each poet's writing and performance with scorecards, just like an Olympic event, and if the judges liked what they heard, you could win the evening's grand prize of fifty bucks.

As it turns out, Austin was the perfect town for my writing. I won a lot of those weekly competitions and would go on to become the Austin Slam Champion three times. I also represented Austin several times at the National Poetry Slam, where I met a slew of other talented writers and performers, many of whom are still my friends today.

I stopped competing in poetry slams in 2001, but that same year I released a self-published chapbook of all my slam poems titled *The Importance of Being Ernest*. I ran off copies on the printer at my day job and stapled them together myself. I also self-produced a CD collection of my slam recordings titled *Ultraman is Airwolf*. Selling my homemade CDs and chapbooks at local shows and on my website made me feel like a one-man punk rock band, and it also helped me make my rent more than once. But most importantly, the response I got from putting my writing out into the world did wonders for my self-esteem, and it gave me the confidence to continue to pursue my dream of becoming a screenwriter and a novelist.

Around the same time, I began to post my work on the Internet, and that's when crazy things started to happen. Several of my recordings went viral, eventually becoming bona fide memes. The text of "When I Was A Kid" has been posted and forwarded (alas, often without my name attached) around the Internet thousands of times. In fact, I just Googled the first line of that poem in quotes and it returned nearly one million hits! My suggestion about using *Airwolf* as an adjective is now an entry in the Urban Dictionary. And my most popular slam poem, "Dance Monkeys Dance," has been translated into over thirty languages and adapted into a viral video with millions of views on YouTube.

The high point of my new Internet pseudo-fame came when geek icon Wil Wheaton discovered my slam recordings and posted a link to them on the popular website Fark, which helped me sell hundreds of books and CDs. A few years later, Cory Doctorow did the same thing when he posted a link to "Nerd Porn Auteur" on the immensely popular geek website Boing Boing. In fact, those are the reasons why I would later make Cory Doctorow and Wil Wheaton the President and VP of the future Internet in my novel *Ready Player One*. It was my way of saying thank you to both of them for sharing my stuff.

Although it has now been over a decade since these poems were first written and performed, I'm still proud of them. I think most of them still hold up pretty well, and serve as great time capsule for who I was —as a person and a writer—during that time in my life. If you dig reading them on the page, feel free to pop over to ernestcline.com, where you can download recordings of many of these pieces for free.

Thank you for reading, and for being so Airwolf.

MTFBWYA,

Ernie Cline

Austin, TX

July 2013

WHEN I WAS A KID

When I was a kid
adults used to bore me to tears
with their tedious diatribes about how hard things used to be
when they were growing up,
what with walking twenty-five miles to school every morning,
uphill, both ways, through year-round blizzards,
carrying their younger siblings on their back
to their one-room schoolhouse
where they maintained a straight-A average,
despite their full-time after-school job
at the local textile mill
where they worked for .35 cents an hour
just to help keep their family from starving to death.

And I remember promising myself that, when I grew up,
there was no way in hell
I was going to lay a bunch of crap like that on kids
about how hard I had it and how easy they've got it.

But now that I've reached the ripe old age of 28...
I can't help but look around and notice
that the youth of today—
You've got it so fucking easy!
I mean, compared to my childhood,
you live in a goddamn Utopia!
And I hate to say it, but you kids today,
"You don't know how good you've got it."

I mean, when I was a kid...

We didn't have the Internet.
If we wanted to know something,
we had to go to the goddamn library and look it up!
And there was no email!
You had to actually write someone a letter,
with a pen,
and then you had to walk all the way across the street

and put it in the mailbox.
And it would take, like, a week to get there.

And there were no MP3s or file sharing!
If you wanted to steal music
you had to go down to the record store and shoplift it yourself!
Or you had to wait around all day and tape it off of the radio,
and then the DJ would usually talk over the beginning
and fuck it all up!

You wanna hear about hardship?

You couldn't just download porn.
You had to bribe some homeless dude
to buy you a copy of *Hustler* from the 7-11.
It was either that or jack off to the lingerie section
of the JC Penny catalog.
Those were your options!

And there was no call waiting! If you were on the phone
and someone else called—
they got a freakin' busy signal!

And we didn't have Caller ID either!
When the phone rang, you had no idea who it was!
It could be your boss, a collection agency, your mom,
your drug dealer—you didn't know!
You had to just pick it up and take your chances, mister!

And we didn't have any fancy Sony PlayStation video games
with high-resolution 3D graphics.
We had the Atari 2600
with games like Space Invaders and Asteroids.
and the graphics sucked ass!
Your guy was just a square!
You had to use your imagination!
And there were no multiple levels or screens.
It was just one screen, forever,
and you could never win.

The game just kept getting harder and faster until you died. Just like life!
Those video games built character, Sonny Jim!

And when you went to the movie theater—
there was no such thing as stadium seating!
All the seats were the same height.
If a tall guy sat in front of you, you were screwed!

And sure, we had cable, but we still only got, like, 20 channels!
And there was no on-screen menu!
You had to use a little book called the *TV Guide* to find out what was on!

And there was no Cartoon Network!
You could only get cartoons on Saturday morning!

Do you see what I am saying?!
We had to wait all week!
You spoiled little bastards!

See, that's the problem with you kids today.
You've got it too damn easy!
You're spoiled!

I swear to god, you wouldn't last five minutes...
Back in 1987.

THE GEEK WANTS OUT

At first glance
I probably appear to be a somewhat ordinary,
somewhat average looking fellow.
Calm, harmless, at ease.

But this is by design.
You see, it is through decades of research and rigorous training
that I have crafted this façade of normalcy.

And now, through intense concentration,
I am able to function in a social setting.
I can speak at length with educated people about
pertinent matters of public importance,
such as literature,
or the current political climate in Europe.

I am capable of conversing with you
without ever revealing that just underneath the surface
of this manufactured veneer
there hides an altogether different person.
A monster, some might say.
My alter-ego.
He is the opposite of the image I project.
He is the antithesis of Cool.
He is the last person you want to get
trapped in a conversation with.

He is The Geek.
The obsessive science fiction movie watching,
comic book collecting,
Monty Python dialogue memorizing,
Dungeons and Dragons playing GEEK
that I struggle daily to keep hidden from the world.

But The Geek Wants Out.

He want to talk to you.
He wants to give you his doctoral dissertation on why
The Adventures of Buckaroo Banzai Across the 8th Dimension
is the greatest fucking film of all time!

He wants to bitch slap you because
you've never seen *Big Trouble in Little China.*
What? Have you been living in a fucking cave?!

He wants to kick your ass in *Star Wars* Trivial Pursuit.
And he will.
Because he's a fucking Geek.

And he wants his toys.
He wants the complete set
in mint condition,
still in the box.

He wants every item on the planet
that is even remotely related to Ultraman.
Because Ultraman is Airwolf!

He could give a squirt of piss
about sports or politics or rhetoric.
Such things are of no consequence to him.
What matters is the release date of the
next *Lord of the Rings* movie!

You see, The Geek can't wait.
The Geek has no patience.
He wants what he wants when he wants it.
And all he wants is stupid shit!

He wants his own TARDIS.
He wants his own light saber.
He wants to buy a DeLorean.
And he wants to drive it 88 miles per hour.

He wants movies.
He wants to see the Director's Cut.
He wants the impossible to find Japanese bootleg with
6 minutes of never-before-seen footage.

He wants to watch *Blade Runner*. Again.
He wants to watch *Brazil*. Again.
He wants to watch *A Clockwork Orange*.
Again and Again!

But I deprive him of these things, as best I can,
until I can no longer ignore his voice
screaming in my head.

I am Jekyll. He is Hyde.
I am Bruce Banner. He is the Hulk.
Especially the Hulk from issues #272 to #378.

But no longer!
I am putting a stop to all this nerdy shit right now!
I'm an adult, for Christ's sake!
And this body isn't big enough for the both of us.
One of us has to go, and it's gonna be him.
I banishing the Geek forever to the Phantom Zone,
just like in *Superman II!*
Because, in the end...
there can be only one.

BOTTOM BUNK MESSIAH

The second semester of my sophomore year at college
I shared my dorm room with Jesus Christ,
and I think I can honestly say that I wasn't the least bit trepidatious
about sharing my dorm room with a foreign exchange student
because I figured that anything had to be better than my last roommate:
who was a dim-witted, misogynistic, knuckle-dragging
football-playing business-slash-physical education major
whom I had considered killing
in his sleep
on several occasions,
just to get him out of my room,
out of my life,
and out of the gene pool.
But luckily he was now serving five to fifteen years
on three counts of date rape
at a Cincinnati correctional facility
where, if there is any justice,
he is being sodomized on hourly shifts.

So in comparison, I figured bunking with this low-key Yanni
look-alike from Bethlehem would be a welcome change.

I couldn't have been more wrong.

I first met "The Lord" as he was moving into our dorm room,
and I helped him assemble this rickety-looking entertainment center
that his step-father, a carpenter, had made for him
as a combination birthday-slash-Christmas present.
I immediately sympathized with how bad it must suck having
a birthday that falls right on Christmas, because you know that
everyone is just gonna lump all your presents together.
But he just gave me a confused look and continued to unpack
his wardrobe, which consisted of six togas
and two pairs of Birkenstocks.

In a few weeks, he started to get on my nerves.

First my VHS copy of Monty Python's *Life of Brian* shows up
broken and in the trash.
Like I'm not going to figure out who did that.

Then his friends, or "apostles" as he called them, started to crash
in our room. Just a few of them at first, and only a few nights a week,
but before too long there were TWELVE of these assholes,
and they were sleeping on our floor
seven nights a week.
And one of them was always stealing my Pepsi.
I suspect it was Judas.

After a while, the whole "Son of God" thing
started to go to his head.
He started to get reckless.
He started curing frat boys of their gonorrhea for a nominal fee
to make a little money on the side.

Then one night his girlfriend, a political science major
named Mary Magdalene, had a party.
She only invited about 30 people, but over 200 showed up.
And by then Jesus was already baked off his gourd,
and when the beer ran out
he started turning the tap water into Heineken.
Right in front of everyone.

When people started to complain that there wasn't any food,
he took a few slices of cold pizza out of the fridge,
started tearing them into pieces, and somehow managed to feed
everyone there!

Then our coke-head pal Lazarus ODs on a speedball in the bathroom
 and before anybody can so much as call 9-1-1, Jesus yells
Lazarus, come out!
The guy jumps up without so much as a hangover.
It was like something out of a George Romero movie.

Well, after that, people started to talk.
People start to follow him to class.
He started to give speeches.
He was hip. He was happening. He was popular.
He was "Big Messiah On Campus."
There was talk of a Nike contract.

But that all came to a tragic end on Easter weekend.
When I came back from home I was told the tragic news:
He had been killed in a bizarre fraternity hazing ritual involving
two other pledges, some Romans,
and several expulsions.

Well, naturally, I was upset.
Until they told me that if your roommate dies,
you get straight As across the board in all your classes.

Some people say Christ died for my sins.
All I know is—I got an A in Astronomy.

Of course, after I had told all of my professors to kiss my ass,
Jesus shows up on the south quad three days later,
apparently having faked his own death.

No one ever saw him again after that.
His disciples came and cleared all of his stuff out of our room,
but accidentally left behind a pair
of his Mickey Mouse boxer shorts,
AKA "The Shroud of Turin,"
which I sold to the *National Enquirer* for a cool million.

Maybe he wasn't such a bad roommate after all.

NERD PORN AUTEUR

I've noticed that there don't seem to be any porno movies
that are made for guys like me.

All the porn I've come across was targeted
at beer-swilling, sports bar dwelling alpha males.
Men who like their women stupid and submissive,
men who can only get it up
for monosyllabic cock-hungry nymphos
with gargantuan breasts and a three word vocabulary.

Adult films are populated with these
collagen-injected, liposuctioned women,
many of whom have resorted to surgery and self-mutilation
in an attempt to look the way they have been told to look.
These aren't real women.
They're objects.
And these movies aren't erotic.
They're pathetic.
These vacuum-headed fuck-bunnies don't turn me on.
They disgust me.

And it's not that I'm against pornography.
I mean, I'm a guy.
And guys need porn. Fact.
Like a preacher needs pain,
like a needle needs a vein,
guys need porn.

But I don't want to watch this misogynist
He-man woman-hater porn!

I want porno movies
that are made with guys like me in mind!
Guys who know that the sexiest thing in the world is
a woman who is smarter than you are.

You can have the whole cheerleading squad.
I want the girl in the tweed skirt and the horn-rimmed glasses…
Betty Finnebowski, the valedictorian!

Oh yes.
First, I want to copy her Trig homework
and then I want to make mad passionate love to her
for hours and hours,
until she reluctantly asks if we can stop
because she doesn't want to miss *Battlestar Galactica*.
Summa Cum Laude, baby!
THAT is what I call erotic!

But do you ever see that kind of woman
in a contemporary adult film? *No!*

Which is why I'm gonna start writing and directing geek porno!
I shall be the quintessential nerd porn auteur!

And the women in my porno movies will be
the kind that drive nerds like me mad with desire:

I'm talking about the girls
who used to fuck up the grading curve!
The girls who were in the Latin Club
and the National Honor Society!
Chicks with weird clothes, braces,
four-eyes and 4.0 GPAs!
Brainy, articulate bookworms,
with MENSA cards in their purses and chips on their shoulders!

My porn starlets will come in all shapes and sizes.
My porn starlets will be too busy working on their PhD
to go to the gym.

In my kind of porn movies
the girls wouldn't even have to get naked.
They'd just take the guys down to the rec room
and beat them repeatedly at chess,

and then talk to them for hours
about Heisenberg's uncertainty principle
or the underlying social metaphors in the *Alien* movies.

Buy stock in some hand cream companies
because there is about to be a major shortage!

And I'm not just talking about straight porn, oh no!
There should be fuck films for my nerd brethren
of all sexual orientations! Gay Nerd Porn movies
with titles like *Dungeons and Drag Queens*.

This idea is a fucking goldmine.
I am going to make millions.
Because this country is full
of database programmers and electronics engineers,
and they aren't getting the loving they so desperately need.

And you can help:
If you're an intelligent woman who is interested in
breaking into the Adult Film Industry...
and if you can tell me the name
of Luke Skywalker's home planet,
then you are *hired!*

It doesn't matter if you think you're overweight or unattractive.
It doesn't matter if you don't think you're beautiful...
You are beautiful.
And I will make you a star.

IF NOSTRADAMUS
WERE A GUIDANCE COUNSELOR

Yeah, I know that you're a senior in high school
and that I'm your guidance counselor
and that you're here in my office
seeking some counseling and some guidance
because you're worried about your future
you're terrified of your future
just like every other snot-nosed punk
who comes rolling into my office.

I know, because I sit here all goddamn day
listening to you little shits whine and moan,
expecting ME to make you feel better,
to assuage your fears,
to tell you that once you get out in the real world
everything is gonna be okay.
To say, "Don't worry, Johnny, it's all gonna work out."

Well, I can't do that anymore,
and you know why?!
Because I'm Nostradamus,
and I can SEE into the future
and you're all FUCKED!
You're goddamn SAT scores don't mean shit!
You're doomed!

Do you really want to know what the future holds? Do ya, Johnny?
Because I can tell you!

You're gonna start out by being a below average college student who
rarely shows up for class, smokes a lot of pot, gets a Tasmanian Devil
tattoo, has unprotected sex with countless anonymous partners, gets
arrested for setting fire to the ROTC building, and then drops out
halfway through the last semester of their fifth year to follow Phish
around on tour.

Then you'll wind up spending the next few years as a very successful heroin addict/porn-star who stars in over 430 films, including *Anal Rodeo*, *Romancing the Bone*, and *Edward Penishands*.

This will segue nicely into your first suicide attempt,
a long stay at the methadone clinic, and a three-year stint in the food service industry, after which you'll move back home, where you'll spend the next year lying around on your parent's couch, eating Cheesy Poofs and watching the Discovery Channel.

When given an ultimatum by your parents,
you'll finally go back, finish college, get your degree in Art History, and then run right out and snag yourself a 401k cubicle job at some huge multinational corporation that makes napalm and pesticide so you can pay off all those student loans in a timely fashion, maintain your impeccable credit rating, get yourself a twelve-disc CD changer installed in the trunk of your Toyota Camry, while you wait for your employee stock options to split again so you can buy that 3 bedroom, 2 ½ bath mortgage in the suburbs with a chemically treated lawn and a power leaf-blower.

About this time you'll marry someone you meet at work that
you don't really love, but hey, let's face it, you're not getting any younger. You'll cheat on them out of sheer boredom whenever the opportunity arises, the two of you will crank out a couple of kids for the tax break, you'll get yourself some personalized license plates to make yourself feel special, go into therapy, and start getting gray hair just in time for your mid-life crisis.

At which point you'll realize that you've spent the majority of your adult life deep-throating the corporate cock, without ever doing anything remotely creative, and that when you die the only thing you're gonna leave behind is a pile of empty Prozac bottles and 1.6 children who hate your fucking guts and swear to god that they will never be anything like you.

MR. NOSTRADAMUS
GUIDANCE COUNSELOR

Boom! Perfect time to start your two decade-long stint as an
accomplished functional alcoholic, followed by your divorce, your
second marriage, and your second divorce,
after which you'll move in with your oldest son's family,
and they'll tolerate you until you get so old you start pissing the bed.

Then they'll stick your geriatric ass in some tomb of a retirement
community where you'll live out the remainder of your empty
pathetic miserable life
using denture cream,
battling Alzheimer's Disease,
eating mushy carrots three meals a day,
watching Andy Griffith reruns,
and begging your nurse to kill you.

Actually, I'm just fucking with you, Johnny.
Don't worry. It's all gonna work out.

Cunning Linguistics

I have heard other members of my gender,
in their more philosophic moments—
during living-room, locker-room, road-trip discussions
about Sex
(never Intimacy)
about Fucking
(never Making Love).

As both boy and man I have been witness to these
testosterone-driven debates about the pros and cons
of one or more of the seemingly infinite number of angles
from which it is possible for a man to penetrate a woman.

Because, for most of men, penetration IS sex,
either intercourse
or fellatio
or some combination of the two.
Despite the overwhelming fact that a little less than thirty percent
of the women on THIS particular planet can reach orgasm through
intercourse alone.

But if during one of these dick-swinging diatribes you are to broach
the subject of, god forbid, cunnilingus—
oral sex performed... *on a woman?*—
then it is met with distaste, disinterest, or disregard.
It is dismissed as some cursory act.
Something done only out of reciprocation for a blow-job.
The *She did it to me so I guess I have to do it to her* mentality.

 Or worse yet, it is categorized as some obligatory act of foreplay.
Something done begrudgingly for five minutes to "get her
warmed up for the main event."
As though the act itself were merely a preamble to penetration
and nothing more.

But there are those among my brethren enlightened enough
to see this act for what it truly is.
Not one of subjugation or something to be suffered through.

This is the reception of a sacrament.
This is attacking a woman's desire at its very center.
This is drinking wine right off the vine,
sucking honey right from the hive.
This is about giving, instead of taking.
About caring, instead of conquering.
And this, more often than not, is what she really wants

Now don't get me wrong,
because during intercourse there are moments of unrivaled
rapture and symbiosis.
But ask any honest member of the opposite sex and she's likely to tell you
that a woman cannot live by the bone alone.

You see, what I'm getting at here,
in, pardon the pun, Layman's Terms,
is that that tedious, repetitive thrusting
that you think is driving her wild
is the number one cause of women having to fake their orgasm
just to get you
the hell off
of them.

And nine out of ten French guys will tell you
that just going down on her
is the best way to make sure she comes.

Therein lies the bulk of my message,
my argument,
and my point.
Unenlightened, Neanderthal frat boys
can continue to feign intolerance
at the taste or the smell,
while boasting about the size of their phallus,
all of them leaving a sea of unsatisfied women in their wake.

And that is an unnecessary, intolerable injustice.
Because, fellas...

With just an iota of consideration
this is one problem
we could easily LICK.

Tech Support

Hello, you've reached Technical Support.
Yes, this is Technical Support.
Thank you for calling Technical Support.
This is Ernie.
My name is Ernie.
I am the one they call Ernie.
Ernie speaking.
How may I help you?
How may I help you this evening?
What seems to be the problem?
Is your computer generating an error message?

Well, when did this happen?
How did this happen?
What in the hell did you do to it?
My god, what the fuck have you done?

Relax.
It's cool.
I'll help you.
That's why I'm here.
I'm here to help you.
All day, all night.
Just a big, fat, twitching brain
wired up to a telephone
waiting to answer every goddamn computer-related question
that you have.
You need my help.
And I'm here to help you.
Now, tell me what's wrong.

It's the Internet, right?
You need to get on the Internet.
Booted up,
Jacked in,
Online.
It's imperative.

And I understand.
I mean, after all, the Internet is a revolutionary means of
communication that can decentralize power by providing everyone
with a voice, since it is the only truly free medium of global
information exchange, as it is not controlled by any one organization,
corporation, government, or media cartel.

But you...
You just wanna download pictures
of Gillian Anderson's pussy, right?
You wanna send email.
You wanna send email to Jerry Springer.
You're just dying to visit Stone Cold Steve Austin's website.
The entire world is at your fingertips and this is the best
that you can come up with.
You want stock quotes,
bomb schematics,
bestiality centerfolds.
You want to use the pseudonym "HotCock007' to pick up
Japanese schoolgirls on AOL.
But you can't, can you, Captain Caveman?
Because "Computer is broken."

And the problem could be hardware, software,
fucking Tupperware for all you know.
Christ, you can't even remember your password.
You're in over your head.
You're out of your depth.
You're five kinds of stupid
and you want somebody to hold your hand
and tell you exactly what to do.
Help me, Ernie.
Save me, Ernie.
Fix it, Ernie.
Ernie, kiss my hard drive and make it better.

Relax.
You're in good hands.
I can help you.
The Internet is my bitch.

41

The computer and I are one.
I speak its language.
I'm like fucking TRON.
Domo arigato, Mr. Roboto.

You see, it's manifest destiny.
This is my job.
This is what I do.
The imposition of Order on Chaos.
System on Fact.
Classification on Data.
I measure time in bits, bytes, kilobytes, megabytes, terabytes.
The future has teeth.

And you're seeing all of your worst fears
about technology come true.
Not only is big brother watching you,
he knows your PIN number.
Welcome, my son, to the machine.
Your fate is being decided by forces
that you can't even begin to comprehend
and you feel like a hairless pink fetus
floating in a Plexiglas bathtub
somewhere deep inside The Matrix.

But don't worry, Coppertop.
It's cool.

You've reached Technical Support.
This is Technical Support.
Thank you for calling Technical Support.
This is Ernie
speaking.

THE IMPORTANCE OF BEING ERNEST

Ernest Cline.
That's the name they gave me.
Says so right there on my Birth Certificate.
Typed there with indifference by some blue-haired
gum-popping hospital secretary:
Ernest Cline.

But here in America we like our names to end in a vowel.
So Harolds become Harry.
Jennifers become Jenny.
And the scattered, odd souls name Ernest…
Become Ernie.

ERNIE.
That is the name I learned to answer to.
The name that adults would shout
to summon or scold me.
Ernie is the first word that I ever scrawled on a piece of paper,
all crooked lines in crayon.

Ernie was my name.
Ernie was who I was.
Ernie was me.
And other than being a tad upset that Miss Molly on Romper Room
never included me in the long list of children whose names she saw
through her magic TV mirror,
I had no complaints.
It was a good name.
It was my name.
I was Ernie
and that was cool.

Until that sunny September morning
when I stumbled bright-eyed
out onto that Kindergarten playground
Wearing Coke-bottle glasses,

a bowl haircut,
and proudly displaying my first-day-of-school nametag
on my chest.

You see, I was about to have a little rendezvous with realization
about my name,
here on the asphalt arena of childhood.
Because, you see, THE QUESTION was coming,
and it came in the guise of
red-headed little Billy Spurlock,
who ran up to me by the monkey bars,
pointed his finger at me,
took a deep breath,
and became the first
of a million or so children (of all ages)
to ask me the rhetorical question:
"Hey Ernie!! Where's Bert?!"

And I had no comeback,
no retort,
no witty reply.
Because, you see, his parents had wisely given him the
innocuous name of William.
Perhaps named after Bill the Bard Shakespeare,
who first posed the question:
What's in a name?

What's in a name?
Well, I can tell you what's in a name,
If, like me, your name happens to be ERNIE
and that happens to be a name that you share
with a freakish orange closeted homosexual muppet
with a rubber-ducky fetish who lives in passionate Mappelthorpean
ecstasy with his
yellow banana-headed pigeon-molesting lover BERT...

Well, then your name pretty much guarantees that every
tweedle-brained double-digit IQ asshole you run into on the street
is gonna ask you that same question
over and over,

with the occasional reference to Big Bird
or the Cookie Monster.

But by the time I hit junior high,
words had become my weapons,
and I had an answer, several answers to that question:

"Hey Ernie! Where's Bert?"
"I think he's down at the bus station getting a five-dollar blow-
job from your father. You know, daddy has to pay for that crack
somehow."

"Hey Ernie! Where's Bert?"
"Bert? I believe he's off making another all-anal porno movie with
your mom. BERT BONES SUBURBAN BIMBOS IN THE
BACK DOOR – VOLUME TWELVE?"

But I don't react that way anymore, and I'll tell you why:

A few years ago I got on a Greyhound bus in California
and I sat down next to a guy who introduced himself as Linus.

This guy's first name was LINUS.

And after about a millisecond of hesitation,
I turned to him and said:
"Hey, Linus. Where's your blanket?"

Then I introduced myself.
"Pleased to meet you, Linus.
My name...is Billy."

Curriculum Vitae

I've never been much good at selling myself,
which is probably why I rank Job Interviews right up there with,
oh, say, Chinese Water Torture on my list of fun things to do.
I think I'd rather chew broken glass
at a Menudo Reunion Concert
being held in the third concentric circle of Dante's Inferno
than suffer the agony of auditioning myself
in some sanitized office
for some well-groomed stranger
who is intent on dissecting my identity
to match an eighty-word
computer-generated job description
while I sit there fidgeting and trying desperately to remember
which parts of my resume are actually true.

But I do my best to dodge the barrage of calculated, probing
questions strategically designed to lay my soul bare for easy corporate
analysis:

"What makes you think you're qualified for this position?"
"What skills do you possess that set you apart from the other applicants?"
and the dreaded, inevitable:
"Tell me why I should hire YOU!???"

Me?
Well…because I'm a hard worker.
I'm dedicated.
I enjoy a challenge.
I enjoy working with people.
I work well independently.
I work well as part of a group.
I can give orders, I can take orders.
I show up on time. Hell, I usually show up early.
I have good personal hygiene.
I have a Can-Do attitude.
I'm a Self-Starter…

I've never been convicted of a felony.

I'm over 18, a U.S. Citizen,
and I'm authorized to work in this country.
I can take constructive criticism,
I keep my work space tidy,
I can probably pass your drug-test.

I follow through.
I manage time efficiently.
And I'm proficient with the Internet,
Hypertext Markup Language,
File Transfer Protocols, Microsoft Word,
Windows 3.1, 9x, NT, and
nine-millimeter Beretta Handguns.
I know how to make a thermonuclear device out of
everyday household items.
I know who really shot JFK.

If I wanted to, pal,
I could reach into your chest, pull out your heart,
show it to you while it's still beating,
AND THEN describe its physiological layout, including
the location of the aorta,
and the left and right ventricles.

You see, I've got what it takes.
I've got the world on a string.
I'm ambidextrous.
And I can use words like obsequious and ubiquitous correctly in a sentence.
I can make weapons-grade plutonium
into a yummy casserole.
I can make a difference.
I can locate Botswana on a map.
I can swing dance.
I'm a team player.
And I've been a puppet, a poet, a preacher, a pauper, a pawn, and a king.
I am not now, nor have I ever been, a homosexual,
but I am willing to learn.

I can play "Heart and Soul" on the piano with my toes.
I can bring home the bacon and fry it up in a pan.
I can quote Shakespeare when I'm drunk.
You see, I am the One the Legend spoke of.

I can pull the Sword from the Stone,
hook up free cable, make Denver Omelets,
and program my VCR.

I don't take long lunch breaks,
I don't steal office supplies,
And I rarely, if ever, call in sick.

And in case you're about to ask me if I have any weaknesses…

FUCK NO, I don't have any weaknesses,
unless you count Kryptonite.

I have been known to fly into vengeful fits of homicidal rage when
I get turned down for a job by some self-important, balding,
baby-boomer FUCKHEAD like you.

But other than that, no…

No real weaknesses.

So why don't you climb down off your high horse,
and just give me a yes or no answer, pal.
Because these are just a few of the reasons,
right off the top of my head,
why you
should hire
me.

AIRWOLF

At the dawn of the Paleolithic period
when the first humans left their caves,
mastered the secrets of fire,
and started making tools
with which to hack civilization out of the wilderness—
This was mankind's first, tiny step
toward an unseen, singular goal
that would take millennia to achieve.

The centuries that we spent devising
physics, mathematics, chemistry, engineering, metallurgy—
All of our combined knowledge
and technological advancements as a species
were to finally culminate in the creation of a machine of such flawless
beauty that it now clearly stands out as human civilization's crowning
achievement:

Airwolf.

In 1984 the world's most brilliant scientists and engineers were
assembled in secret for the sole purpose of constructing the world's
most advanced Mach One Plus attack helicopter.
This would be more than just an instrument of war.
It would be a work of art.
And no expense was spared in this,
mankind's boldest endeavor to date.
The original da Vinci parchments were consulted.
Extrapolations were made.
Fifth generation Swiss craftsmen were flown in
merely to assemble the dashboard.

There was painstaking attention to detail.

And upon its completion,
those present were unable to do anything
but stand and marvel
in wonder and in awe

at the sleek, black aerodynamic perfection
that was Airwolf.

And I know there are voices of dissent shouting,
"What about Blue Thunder? What about Knight Rider?"
Fuck Blue Thunder.
Fuck Michael Knight!
And the hell with Street Hawk and Firefox…

AIRWOLF.

Airwolf is the adjective we should use to describe anything
of majesty, beauty, and intensity.
Something that is simply fucking bad ass…is Airwolf.
James Brown's music is Airwolf.
Shakespeare is Airwolf.
Sex so good it makes your spine ache
and your knees buckle…That's Airwolf.

And nothing is more Airwolf than *Airwolf.*

Airwolf is the Holy Grail. The Golden Fleece.
The thing you want that you cannot have.
When you go sprinting through the mall,
desperate to fill the emptiness in your life
through the purchase of name brand clothing and electronics-
You will never achieve satisfaction.
Because the one brand name you really want
is the one you can never have:

Airwolf?

Oh, I'm sorry, we're all sold out.
That item was only available for a very limited time
and in very limited supply.
ONE.
And only one man stepped forward to purchase it.
Stringfellow Hawke!

And he bought it for the bargain basement price
of having the solid brass balls to steal it
from the US government, when, in their hubris,
they were foolish enough to ask him to be the test pilot!

You don't ask a guy with a name like Stringfellow Hawke
to fly your top-secret black helicopter.
Why?
Because he is obviously going to steal it!
He's obviously a prototypical American anti-hero,
for fuck's sake!

He lives in the mountains.
He plays the cello.
His name is *Stringfellow Hawke!*
He cannot be trusted.
He's not gonna use Airwolf to execute
American foreign policy.
He's going to keep it for himself.

Which is exactly what you would do.

Walking out to your back yard
to stare at it every night around sunset.
The sight of it filling you with such peace and resonant satisfaction
that you would come to believe the perfect haiku would have just
two syllables:

Airwolf.

PICK SIX

6:30am alarm clock
like an intermittent swarm of Nazi hornets
that just rips you awake
with pre-programmed electronic indifference out of the
450 degree Fahrenheit dream you were having
about animalistic sex on top of Stonehenge
with someone passionate and European.
Awake to a weekday.
It's a fucking weekday.

And you slap that snooze button like a hemophiliac
going after a two-pound mosquito sucking on his neck—
and are granted an eight-minute reprieve.

Which turns out to be just long enough for you
to contemplate the fact
that your will no longer seems to be your own.
I mean, it's not like you want to get up out of bed,
but you have to,
because you have financial responsibilities
that necessitate gainful employment.
Needs and desires,
needs and desires
with enough pull to drag you stumbling into the shower spray
as you recite this litany of want:

I will trade them little pieces of my life in eight-hour chunks
for which I will receive in return Legal Tender
that I can trade in for goods and services,
food, clothing, cable, cat food, car payments, and candlelight dinners.

This Mantra of Need
sucks you into the metallic insect traffic crawl
into the city,
into the city
amidst a sea of sport utility vehicles and minivans,
like the one in front of you

that is owned by the proud parent of an honor student
who has chosen to pontificate from their rear bumper
their opinion
that *Jesus Saves* and *Abortion Stops a Beating Heart.*

And you realize at that moment that you think so little
of your present set of circumstances
that it just might be worth scrapping it all
to walk up there
yank them out of their Aerostar
and stop their beating heart.

And you think about doing it.
You actually stop…
and think about doing it.

But then reason returns, as it always does
and you opt instead for just averting your eyes…
Which fall on a billboard.
A familiar, ominous black billboard
with white numbering
that displays an amount so huge
that your mind can't quit grasp its immensity:

FORTY-TWO MILLION DOLLARS
STATE LOTTO
PICK-SIX

And the reasonable side of you just shrugs it off and continues
on with its imperative mission of just getting you
to your fucking job.

But the other half,
the wild-eyed eccentric,
sees an answer,
sees an escape,
sees a way out,
sees a rat-race rip-cord that you can pull to
eject yourself out of the whip-saw cycle of production
and consumption that your life has become.

It grabs you by the shirt collar,
slams you up against the wall, and says:
"I want a ticket
and I want a shot at that forty-two mil, pal!!"

And that voice haunts you all day long at the office
as you half-heartedly converse
with customers, clients, and co-workers,
all who seemed to be engaged in activities
that have NOTHING TO DO with being ALIVE.
It haunts you on the drive home until you find yourself
in the unlikeliest of circumstances:
Seeking salvation at the Circle K.

Pencil in hand, a revelation:
If I can just make the right six marks
on this piece of paper
I will be captain of my soul again.
And you hand them to the vacant-eyed clerk
along with a one-dollar bill,
which in terms of your job
is equal to 4.5 minutes of your life,
and in return he hands you a ticket
and an astronomical possibility
which you pocket and forget about
until the following Sunday night
when you realize:

You have to get up again and go to work in the morning.

And this despairing thought sends you
in search of the Sunday paper
amidst thoughts of winning,
visions of winning
and calling your boss at home to quit your job in a flurry
of righteous indignation and colorful profanity
and then calling each one of your friends
and letting them know
that they don't have to go to work in the morning either.

Because you're all going on a year-long trip around the world
on a wave of Ben-Franklin-Green
at the end of which you'll buy a house on the ocean
with a hundred and ten rooms
and a hundred and ten channels of cable
where you can all live Happily Ever After.

CURTAINS

You probably think you're immortal, don't you?

Perhaps not in the literal sense, no.
But when you think about dying,
if you think about it at all,
I'll bet you tell yourself
that you have all the time in the world.
You're still pretty young.
And death isn't something you need to concern yourself
with for a very long time.

And if you were to imagine the moment of your death,
you'd probably envision yourself at the wizened old age of eighty-seven.
Lying in a warm, king-sized bed,
surrounded by all of your children and grandchildren.
All your goals accomplished,
all your dreams realized.
You are tired, at peace, and ready for the end
when it finally comes.

Yeah. Maybe it'll happen like that.

But then again,
maybe you won't make it home tonight.

Maybe you'll be sitting at a stoplight,
Singing along with Kenny Loggins on the radio,
Everybody cut Footloose!
and BAM!
Out of nowhere you are broadsided by a drunk
in a green 1979 Chevy Malibu.
You die instantly,
and you never know what hit you.

This happens every day.
It just hasn't happened to you yet.

Or maybe it'll be the Big C that gets you.
Melanoma, carcinoma, non-Hodgkin's lymphoma.
Cancer doesn't care how old you are.
Maybe leukemia.
Maybe pneumonia.
Maybe E. coli in the local water supply.

Maybe there will be a fire.
Maybe there will be complications during your appendix removal.

Maybe your heart will stop working properly.

Maybe you'll be flying home for your father's funeral
and your plane will have hydraulic failure
and your family will wait an extra day
and bury you and your father together.
And they'll save a shit load on flowers.

Or it could be food poisoning.
Dismemberment.
Let's not rule out dismemberment.
You might be murdered.
People get murdered.
For revenge. Or money. Or love.
Or sometimes for no reason at all.

You might be an innocent bystander.

Maybe you'll be crushed against the stage
at an Air Supply concert.
But I doubt it.

Maybe the roof of your church will collapse on Sunday morning
and kill you along with the rest of the congregation.

Maybe you won't look both ways
before crossing the street.
Maybe you'll bleed to death on the way to the hospital.
Maybe you'll have an accident.
Accidents will happen.

Maybe your hairdryer will electrocute you.
Maybe the state of Texas will electrocute you.

Eventually, Death is gonna ask you to dance.
And whether you like it or not,
you will do the Mortal Coil Shuffle.
Don't kid yourself.
Your days are numbered.
And all of your plans are subject to change.

126 people have died since I started talking.
Do you think they were all ready for it?
Do you think they all saw it coming?

Maybe you'll see it coming.

Maybe you'll have time to say goodbye.
To say *I'm sorry*.
Or to say *I love you*.
To say and do all the things that you intend to do
right now, as soon as you get around to it.
First thing tomorrow.

CINÉMA VÉRITÉ
(my closing argument)

Ladies and gentlemen of the jury,
Before you rush to judgment
and convict me of cold-blooded murder
please, allow me to say a few words in my own defense.

Because I am not a killer
and I value human life.
Which is why you have to believe me when I tell you
that all three of the people I killed
in that movie theater –
Each and every one of them…deserved to die.

Now, the prosecution would have you believe
that these were premeditated crimes
perpetrated by some bloodthirsty madman.
But this is not the case.

I was just there to watch and enjoy the film
like almost everyone else.
Now, I couldn't tell you
why my three so-called "victims" were there,
but it sure as hell wasn't to watch the goddamn movie!

Let's go over the "body-count," shall we?

Victim #1 – The inconsiderate fuck with the cell phone.
This stupid bastard not only left his cell phone ON during the movie,
but when it rang, he fucking answered it!
And then he proceeded to conduct his little business call right there
  in the theater, so that all the rest of us could listen in.

I think you'll agree, he had to be killed.

So I followed him out to the men's room,
where I strangled him with his own Dilbert necktie.
And I'd do it again.

Victim #2 – The asshole with the laser-pointer.
I come back from the can to find that someone is anonymously
shining a little red laser dot around on the movie screen. Taking
pleasure in ruining the film for everyone. He might as well have been
pissing on the Mona Lisa. Unfortunately for him, he happened to be
sitting directly in front of me.

I think you'll agree, he had to be killed.

So I leaned forward and snapped his neck like a fucking twig. And in
doing so, I made the world a better place.

And finally – Victim #3 –
Yes, I did it.
I killed the white trash woman with the screaming child.
How can I justify such a heinous act?
I'll tell you how.

Because I, and all the other film-lovers in the audience that night,
did not pay eight bucks a piece to listen to her infant scream
for two hours.
But, did she consider that?
No.
Did she take him out to the lobby?
No.
Did it occur to her inbred ass that bringing a 2 year old
to an R-rated movie on a Friday night was not a good idea?
No.
It did not.

Therefore, I think you'll agree—she had to die.

So I did the obvious thing—
I asphyxiated her with her own Twizzlers.
And then
I quietly carried the child out to the lobby myself.

And if I hadn't immediately been arrested for a triple homicide,
I would have taken her orphaned son
and lovingly raised him as my own.

I would have taken him to a movie matinee every weekend,
teaching him to both love and respect the cinema
and to treasure film as one of our most stirring
and accessible art forms.

Because nothing has the power to move and enlighten the masses
like the flickering vicarious light of moving pictures.
If everyone would just shut the fuck up
and watch the goddamn film.

So, ladies and gentleman of the jury,
if it is a crime to love the movies…
Well, then I am guilty as charged.

Will Robinson's Blues Haiku

All through puberty
I've been Lost in Space with my
Mom and two sisters

Footloose Haiku

Small town Christians are
no match for Kenny Loggins
and Kevin Bacon

Galaga Haiku

To defend earth from
the evil alien hordes
I need a quarter

DANCE, MONKEYS, DANCE

Orbiting the sun at about ninety-three million miles
is a little blue planet
and this planet is run
by a bunch of monkeys.

Now, the monkeys don't think of
themselves as monkeys.
They don't even think of themselves as animals.
And they love to list all the things
that they think
separate them from the animals:
Opposable thumbs, self-awareness...
They'll use words like
Homo Erectus and *Australopithecus*.

You say Toe-mate-o,
I say Toe-motto.
They're animals all right.
They're monkeys.
Monkeys with high-speed digital fiber optic technology,
but monkeys nevertheless.

I mean, they're clever.
You've got to give them that.
The pyramids, skyscrapers, phantom jets,
the Great Wall of China.
That's all some pretty impressive shit...
for a bunch of monkeys.

Monkeys whose brains have evolved
to such an unmanageable size
that it's now pretty much impossible
for them stay happy for any length of time.

In fact, they're the only animals
that think they're supposed to be happy.
All of the other animals can just be.

But it's not that simple for the monkeys.
You see, the monkeys are cursed with consciousness.
And so the monkeys are afraid.
So the monkeys worry.
The monkeys worry about everything,
but mostly about what all the other monkeys think.
Because the monkeys desperately want to fit in
with the other monkeys.
Which is hard to do,
because a lot of the monkeys seem to hate each other.
This is what really separates them from the other animals.
These monkeys hate.
They hate monkeys that are different.
Monkeys from different places,
monkeys who are a different color—

You see, the monkeys feel alone.
All six billion of them.

Some of the monkeys pay another monkey
to listen to their problems.

Because the monkeys want answers
and the monkeys don't want to die.
So the monkeys make up gods
and then they worship them.
Then the monkeys argue
over whose made-up god is better.
Then the monkeys get really pissed off.
and this is usually when the monkeys decide
that it's a good time
to start killing each other.

So the monkeys wage war.
The monkeys make hydrogen bombs.
The monkeys have got their whole fucking planet
wired up to explode.
The monkeys just can't help it.

Some of the monkeys play to a sold out crowd...
of other monkeys.

The monkeys make trophies
and then they give them to each other.
Like it means something.

Some of the monkeys think
that they have it all worked out.
Some of the monkeys read Nietzsche.
The monkeys argue about Nietzsche
without giving any consideration to the fact
that Nietzsche
was just another fucking monkey.

The monkeys fall in love.
The monkeys make plans.
The monkeys fuck
and then they make more monkeys.

The monkeys make music
and then the monkeys dance.
Dance, monkeys, dance.

The monkeys make a hell of a lot of noise.
Exhibit A
Monkey making noise.
And when he's done,
five other randomly selected monkeys
will rate this monkey's noises
on a scale from one to ten.
At the end of the night,
they add all the numbers up
to see which monkey made the best noises.

As you can see...
these are some fucked up monkeys.

These monkeys are at once the ugliest
and most beautiful creatures on the planet.

And the monkeys don't want to be monkeys.
They want to be something else.

But they're not.

73

ABOUT THE AUTHOR

Ernest Cline was active in the Austin Poetry Slam from 1997-2001, which is when he wrote all of the stuff in this book. Since then, he has written the screenplay for the cult hit film, *Fanboys* (2009) and the *New York Times* best-selling novel, *Ready Player One* (2011), whose film rights were bought by Warner Brothers. His next novel, *Armada*, will be published by Random House in 2014. He lives in Austin, TX, where he devotes a large portion of his time to geeking out.

For more information, please visit www.ernestcline.com.

ACKNOWLEDGMENTS

My sincere thanks go out to Oscar Wilde, George Carlin, Bill Hicks, Kurt Vonnegut, Jim Henson, Eric Bogosian, Jan Michael Vincent, Ernest Borgnine, Ernest Hemingway, Shin Hayata, Cristin O'Keefe Aptowicz, Derrick Brown, Gary Musgrave, Len Peralta, Steve Marsh, Shappy Seasholtz, Susan Somers-Willett, Mike Henry, and everyone else who used to sling words with me back in the day at the Austin Poetry Slam. Y'all are Airwolf.

IF YOU LIKE ERNEST CLINE, ERNEST CLINE LIKES...

The Year of No Mistakes
Cristin O'Keefe Aptowicz

I Love Science!
Shanny Jean Maney

Songs from Under the River
Anis Mojgani

What Learning Leaves
Taylor Mali

The Undisputed Greatest Writer of All Time
Beau Sia

WRITE BLOODY BOOKS

CPSIA information can be obtained
at www.ICGtesting.com
Printed in the USA
FSOW02n2207021017
39214FS